PARENTING IS F✳✳✳ING HARD

Eat Out in London With Kids

(without losing your mind
or their appetite)

Written by
EMMY WA

HOXTON MINI PRESS

Hazel, (age 3), with Martin (age undisclosed) Koya Ko (p.70)

Parenting is f**king hard

**...so give yourself a break
and go to a f**king nice restaurant**

Before Ann and I had kids, eating out was a delight. It was kingly. After we had kids it was ketchup. The speed at which dining in town went from being a pleasure to being a pain was almost as fast as forks clattered to the floor and the flecks of pudding landed on our pullovers.

Since then, we have – through some effort – discovered a handful of places that not only serve REALLY good food, but they also do it in a way that kids will enjoy. That may be because there is a spiral slide in the dining room, or it may be because the waiters are not angry but extremely nice about a tiny guest who screams. Either way, don't tell anyone else about these places as there is nothing worse than a really lovely restaurant full of noisy kids.

Unless they are your own.

Martin & Ann (with Olive & Hazel)

Granary Square Brasserie (p.44)

Megan's (p.52)
Opposite: Lina Stores (p.152)

Best For...

Meeting non-parent friends

Mouth-watering cocktails, cool decor and amusements spanning arcade games and comic books make Mama Shelter (p.80) the ideal spot for brunch with old friends and offspring. For dinner, try The Arber Garden (p.128), where you can chinwag over upscale pub fare and bloody Marys while the wee ones tackle the kids' activity sheet.

Special occasions

When it comes to fine dining, you can't top Apricity (p.138), a sustainable spot that welcomes even the dinkiest of diners with its children's tasting menu. Or head to the swanky OXO Tower Restaurant (p.110), where fabulous three-course feasts, attentive service and breath-taking views will wow guests big and small.

Older kids

Few pubs are as family-friendly as BrewDog (p.100) in Waterloo, which offers kids' 'Hoppy Meals' as well as mini bowling and a huge tunnel slide to keep bigger ones busy while they wait. Meanwhile, sushi spot inamo's (p.20) interactive tables allow diners to draw, play games and even spy on the kitchen via webcam.

Afternoon tea

Peppa Pig fans will go bonkers for Brigit's Bakery's themed bus tour (p.22), which includes a piglet-friendly spread of sandwiches, scones and cakes served on a customised bus. Or, for something a little more sophisticated, head to Petersham Nurseries (p.154) for a rustic children's tea served in the magical garden Teahouse.

Weekend brunch

Dishoom's (p.32) naan rolls and bottomless chai are the stuff of breakfast legend, and there's even a separate menu for smaller patrons. Meanwhile, Where the Pancakes Are (p.94) offers an all-day mix-and-match menu of pancake stacks topped with whatever sweet and/or savoury treats they desire – no combination is too revolting.

Fussy eaters

Pasta and kids are always a winning combination, and Lina Stores' (p.152) off-menu selection of fresh shapes with homemade sauces should satisfy even the pickiest palates. Or try Wahaca (p.90) for deconstructed DIY taco platters that give kids control over their chow.

Hyperactive tots

Japanese cafe Toconoco's (p.40) cute kitchen play area makes lunch with tiny ones a breeze, while Sweet Thursday's (p.34) giant Duplo box should keep them occupied while their pizza is prepared. Or head to The Hub (p.78), whose playground-adjacent location makes it perfect for kids who simply cannot sit still.

Trying new things

Choice abounds at Seven Dials Market (p.12), whose copious street food vendors spanning countless cuisines encourage the whole family to eat adventurously. And if you thought vegan food was just for grown-ups, head to Mildreds (p.60) and prepare to be wowed by their deliciously different child- (and animal-) friendly eats.

Pull up a highchair and tuck in

A whole book on where to take kids out to eat? Surely just heading down to the nearest Nando's and strapping on a nosebag full of nuggets will do the job? Believe me, I'm a huge advocate of the odd fast food fix – peri-peri chicken-based or otherwise. But haven't you ever longed for something a little more… sophisticated? Maybe some place where you don't have to fill your own drinks, or collect your own cutlery? I'm not necessarily talking Michelin stars, but even something vaguely approaching the kind of dining experiences my partner and I enjoyed pre-kids wouldn't go amiss once in a while. What makes the places in this book great is that they don't just appeal to adults who want a seasonal small plate, your kids will also love them. While you might have assumed your fine-dining days were done the moment you traded all-night parties for nappies, they don't have to be.

It was a great privilege to try out some of the capital's top restaurants with my family while researching this book. But it also had the potential to resemble a special form of torture, in part because my 4-year-old daughter is probably the fussiest, messiest eater I've ever met in my life. Mercifully, my little monster surprised me with her willingness to try new things and her capacity for being, if not quite *charming* company, at least slightly less disgusting than she is at home. Which just proves that kids are often a lot more adaptable than we give them credit for and that maybe the combination of extra-delicious food and slightly more plush surrounds can turn even a fussy eater into a little foodie.

This book might surprise you too. When I started writing it, I was convinced that there was a very specific formula for what constituted a child-friendly restaurant, and it mostly involved crayons and a kids' menu. The more places we visited, however, the more I realised that, while these little extras are always a bonus, they're rarely what makes a meal out with kids truly magical. More often than not, that magic is conjured by people: be it the exceptionally kind or accommodating waiter, or the chef who whipped something up off-menu to appease your picky piccolo. Half the time, kids don't even need 'kids' stuff', they just need a bit of compassion. Although, that said, the place with the giant helter skelter and indoor ice cream truck (p.100) went down pretty well.

What this book *isn't* is a catalogue of all the obvious chain restaurants and overpriced tourist-baiting 'family cafes'. What it *is*, is a lovingly curated list of places you would likely very happily dine at without kids (with the possible exception of the Peppa Pig bus (p.22)), but that you could equally rock up at, tiny terrors or surly teens in tow, and be greeted with highchairs and changing mats, or even board games and screens – and not a whiff of hostility. It is probably a bit more gastronomically diverse than you might expect of a book aimed at families. But have faith; kids are often more adventurous than we give them credit for, too. While researching this book, my otherwise beige-food-obsessed children cheerfully tucked into broccoli tempura at a Japanese cafe (p.40) and rhubarb granita at a low waste restaurant (p.138). The secret? Honestly, I have no idea. But if I can take my family to a nice restaurant and live to tell the tale, I promise you can too.

Emmy Watts,
London

Seven Dials Market

Fun food hall in a former banana warehouse

Parents of fussy eaters, rejoice! Central London's coolest food hall might be a haven for Zoomers with its trendy street-food stalls and novelty dining concepts, but it's also perfect for faddy kids, who'll go bananas for its playful decor (which is themed around, uh... bananas), multitude of delectable cuisines and regular craft sessions from The Kids' Table. The fact that you can pick and mix dishes from multiple vendors makes the market particularly great for families, who can load up on kid-appeasing pizzas (from Bad Boy), heavenly hummus and pittas (from Shuk) and the ooziest cheese toasties (from Pick & Cheese) while the grown-ups get their flavour fix in the form of Truffle's frankly filthy burgers and Yum Bun's fluffy bao bombs. For afters, head to Cucumber Alley for all the melty Taiwanese wheelcakes, gooey crème brûlée crêpes and creamy soft serve their hearts (and bellies) desire.

NEARBY

The Royal Opera House's fun-packed Family Sundays should fuel their appetites (sign up to the mailing list to be the first in the queue for tickets).

DETAILS

Facilities: Highchairs, baby change, kids' menu
Address: 35 Earlham Street, WC2H 9LD
Station: Covent Garden
Web: sevendialsmarket.com

Gloria

Maximalist trattoria

Ever tried to explain the 1990s to your children but concluded that you really had to be there? Well, at Gloria you *can* be there, albeit in a very specific, absurdly camp version where you're eating Neapolitan pizza surrounded by novelty plates. But while this kitsch trattoria might be eerily reminiscent of the 'nice' restaurants you frequented in your youth, you can guarantee the food here is a million times better, even if you're plumping for a margherita pizza – which your kids may well do, and should. Other kid- (and adult-) friendly options include a perfect cacio e pepe, a near-insurmountable lasagne and pretty much anything on the very theatrical, very Italian dessert menu, be it an indulgent dessert pizza oozing chocolate spread or a 6 inch-high slice of lemon meringue pie – something our own childhood memories are sadly lacking.

NEARBY

It's impossible to visit Shoreditch without a browse in Luna & Curious, a mini department store stocking stylish clothing and gifts for women and kids. Or head to Brick Lane or Rivington Street for inspiring street art from the likes of Stik and Thierry Noir.

DETAILS

Facilities: Highchairs, baby change
Address: 54–56 Great Eastern Street, EC2A 3QR
Station: Old Street
Web: bigmammagroup.com/ gloria

RedFarm

Dim sum with a big sense of fun

'Don't play with your food' is not a sentence you'll get away with uttering at this hip-but-cosy dim sum joint, whose Pac-Man dumplings, almond-sprigged porcupine wantons and soup-filled buns speared with red-and-white straws all beg to be toyed with. Such kitsch cuisine may generally be the reserve of more cheap-and-cheerful establishments, but RedFarm's scran is well worth splashing out on, offering style *and* substance that will delight young and old. Novelty dishes aside – because ordering those should be compulsory where kids are concerned – the chunky cheeseburger spring rolls, faultless fried rice, and moreish chicken-and-prawn lollipops are all well suited to young tastes, while the famous pastrami egg rolls and crispy kale cutlets will appease more refined ones. Dessert, should you choose to order it (and, of course, you should), is an irresistible steamed dough volcano oozing molten puddles of vanilla magma.

NEARBY

There's no end of fun to be had in Covent Garden, from themed soft play and vintage vehicles at the London Transport Museum to action-packed family days at the Royal Opera House and world-class exhibitions at Somerset House.

DETAILS

Facilities: Highchairs, baby change
Address: 9 Russell Street, WC2B 5HZ
Station: Covent Garden
Web: redfarmldn.com

inamo

Pan-Asian favourite with interactive tables

While its low lighting and glossy decor might scream 'adults only', this cool sushi spot is actually one of the most child-friendly places to grab dinner in central London. Inamo offers no children's menu as such, but since it almost exclusively serves small plates of tot-pleasing sushi and Asian tapas, it doesn't need to. Good options for dinky diners include a comforting katsu curry, sweet strawberry sushi and a dragon roll that lives up to its name thanks to some clever assembly, while a punchy Bang Bang Cauliflower and tongue-teasing Heaven and Hell Roll should sate more sophisticated palettes. Between (and, let's face it, during) courses, Inamo's pioneering tabletop technology allows diners to play retro games, keep an eye on the kitchen via webcam, and even order dishes and request the bill, which helps keep the service speedy (and the meltdown risk low).

NEARBY

London Transport Museum boasts a stamper trail, themed play area and tons of vintage vehicles. In the summer months, the Somerset House fountains are easily the coolest spot in the capital, while St. Giles Churchyard is home to one of the only good playgrounds in zone 1.

DETAILS

Facilities: Highchairs, baby change, kids' menu
Address: 11–14 Hanover Place, WC2E 9JP
Station: Covent Garden
Also in: Soho
Web: inamo-restaurant.com

Peppa Pig Afternoon Tea Bus

Themed tea for little piggies

Ever had the overwhelming desire to traverse central London on a double-decker bus, taking in the sights while ingesting a Peppa Pig-themed cream tea to the sound of The Bing Bong Song? Probably not. But maybe your toddler has – and that's really who this tea with a twist is aimed at. Dreamt up by the team at Brigit's Bakery, this tot-friendly tour swings by hotspots including Tower Bridge, the Houses of Parliament and Trafalgar Square, while a table-mounted screen tracks your journey via an animated map. Passengers can 'pig' out on generously filled finger sandwiches, miniature scones, cupcakes and Peppa-shaped biscuits, all appealingly presented on specially decorated tables. You don't get to meet Peppa herself, but you *do* get a souvenir cup and activity pack to take home, making this a must for die-hard fans (at least, provided they don't get travel-sick).

NEARBY

Somerset House is always worth a wander thanks to its brilliant programme of cutting-edge exhibitions. Or head to the Artist's Garden on top of Temple tube station for unusual art installations in a serene setting.

DETAILS

Facilities: Kids' toilet onboard
Address: Somerset House, Strand, WC2R 1LA
Station: Temple
Web: b-bakery.com

Cafe Murano

La dolce vita on home turf

This elegant Italian might not be your average family pasta joint, with its leather banquettes, theatre-going clientele and Michelin-star chef, but that doesn't mean that kids aren't welcome. On the contrary, Angela Hartnett's swanky cafe – which, strictly speaking, isn't really a cafe – even offers its youngest diners a special two-course menu, which doubles as an absorbing activity sheet to keep them busy while they wait. This menu perfectly encapsulates Hartnett's vision of 'really good simple, tasty food' with its choice of fresh pasta shapes and sauces, or chicken Milanese in a delectably crisp crumb. Likewise, the adult menu stars unpretentious yet indulgent delights including creamy clam risotto, rich rabbit ragù and comforting lamb parmigiana, concluding with all the tiramisu and panna cotta your appetite will allow.

NEARBY

The only transport you'll need to reach the London Transport Museum is your feet (it's roughly two minutes' walk from the restaurant). Or head to Benjamin Pollock's Toyshop in search of pop-up toy theatres and other retro delights.

DETAILS

Facilities: Highchairs, baby change, kids' menu

Address: 36 Tavistock Street, WC2E 7PB

Station: Covent Garden

Also in: St James's, Bermondsey

Web: cafemurano.co.uk

Barbican Kitchen

Waterside canteen in a Brutalist arts centre

Like the much revered homes in the concrete complex that hosts it, this iconic cafe is at once oddly beautiful, deeply practical and somewhat overpriced – though we'll forgive the latter given that one child eats free with every adult meal purchased. This rather generous deal – along with the upscale canteen vibe and abundance of highchairs – ensures its popularity with families, while its carbon-neutral coffee, build-your-own salads and striking views stop it from veering into kids' club territory. And while the children's selection is small and variable, comprising a couple of satisfying (if stodgy) options served in adorably tiny enamel dishes, staff are generally willing to plate up smaller versions of whatever it is they fancy – supposing mac and cheese is not it. Failing that, you can't go wrong with the handmade pizzas, which are best enjoyed on the lakefront terrace on a balmy summer's day.

NEARBY

Barbican's Squish Space creative play area for under-5s pops up on selected days each week, while the children's library hosts three rhymetime sessions a week. On dry days, head to the Golden Lane Estate's small but brilliant architect-designed playground.

DETAILS

Facilities: Highchairs, baby change, kids' menu
Address: Barbican Centre, Silk Street, EC2Y 8DS
Station: Moorgate
Web: barbican.org.uk

Bread Street Kitchen & Bar

Modern British classics from a celebrity chef

This bustling brasserie may be the brainchild of the eminently sweary Gordon Ramsay, but you needn't fret about its kid-friendly credentials. On the contrary, not only does Bread Street Kitchen offer a Ramsay Kids menu – a recurrent feature across the chef's restaurants – but one under-9 eats free with every adult, with a choice of dependable favourites including bangers and mash, juicy burgers and satisfying bowls of pasta. And while you might think that's the least they can offer given some of the prices – which may well provoke strong language of your own – for the most part it feels justified, with special mentions awarded to the spicy tuna tartare, enormous beef Wellington sharer and an especially excellent bowl of chips. Follow up with the oozing chocolate fondant and prepare to utter more expletives of (ecstatic) disbelief.

NEARBY

Head to the London Mithraeum for a free immersive experience, whereby an ancient Roman temple is reconstructed with smoke, lasers and an enigmatic soundtrack. Just up the road, the Sky Garden offers incredible views of the city via a lush and lofty greenhouse.

DETAILS

Facilities: Highchairs, baby change, kids' menu
Address: One New Change, 10 Bread Street, EC4M 9AJ
Station: Mansion House
Also in: Multiple locations
Web: gordanramsayrestaurants. com

Dishoom

Indian street eats in stylish surrounds

It might be famed for its queues – and we all know how well those go down with kids – but bring a little one (or two) for dinner at this Bombay cafe-inspired spot and you might just manage to skip them altogether. But while priority access isn't always a given, happy little bellies are pretty much guaranteed, whether they opt for a mild murgh or creamy tikka from the kids' selection, or brave something more complex from the small plate-dominated main menu, where fail-safe (little) people pleasers include tangy cheddar-filled naans, an inimitable black daal and sweet kulfi ice lollies. And it's not just dinnertime where Dishoom excels. In fact, its breakfasts are arguably even more legendary, with child-friendly delights including fluffy uttapam pancakes, spicy masala beans on toast and the justifiably hyped naan breakfast roll, washed down with silky lassis all round.

NEARBY

A gambol in the Granary Square fountains is always a winner on warmer days, while the Handyside Gardens playground is perfect for burning off post-feast energy.

DETAILS

Facilities: Highchairs, baby change, kids' menu
Address: 5 Stable Street, N1C 4AB
Station: King's Cross
Also in: Multiple locations
Web: dishoom.com

Sweet Thursday

Friendly neighbourhood Italian

This unpretentious Italian does stress-free family dining so effortlessly you could almost be in a trattoria in Naples enjoying authentically chewy Neapolitan pizza served by actual Italians. As it stands, you're in De Beauvoir Town, but the rest is still true. And while the pizzas are remarkably good – topped with such delights as pea and pistachio pesto and carbonara sauce, and fashioned into fiendishly delicious sandwiches and even friendly bears for the little ones (with the crust twisted into ears) – there's more to this criminally underrated spot than dough. For meat lovers, the Pasta Vesuvio is explosively good (and available in 'bambino' portions) and it's well worth investigating the droolsome dessert menu, starring a naughty Nutella gnocchi and light limoncello-laced mess. Top all that off with a DUPLO corner for between-courses tinkering, and you've got yourself a recipe for an epic meal out.

NEARBY

With its hoard of well-loved ride-on toys and cafe serving up huge pots of tea and homemade cakes, the tranquil Dalston Curve Garden is beloved by locals big and small.

DETAILS

Facilities: Highchairs, baby change
Address: 95 Southgate Road, N1 3JS
Stations: Haggerston, Essex Road
Web: sweetthursday.co.uk

Tonkotsu

Japanese comfort food

Whatever your age, when you're craving comfort, few things hit the spot like a steaming bowl of broth. Tonkotsu – which, incidentally, translates as 'pig bone' – *really* understands broth. In fact, theirs is so restorative, so satisfying and positively joy-giving, it should probably be prescribed by doctors as a miracle cure-all. But let's not forget those slurpably silky homemade noodles. Indeed, just as the sign outside every branch of this fast-growing chain insists, this is *not just a soup shop*, and it has every reason to be proud of its flawlessly chewy udon. Older kids should be happy enough with a regular portion of ramen or katsu, while younger ones will likely appreciate the compartmentalised kids' boxes that let them build their own. And to finish? Nothing quite says comfort like a jelly-filled ice cream sandwich with a rainbow-sprinkle crumb.

NEARBY

Talacre Community Sports Centre offers open-play gymnastics sessions for under-5s on weekdays, while its Treetops soft play structure is always open to all ages. Or head to Kentish Town City Farm for pond dipping and donkey rides.

DETAILS

Facilities: Highchairs, kids' menu
Address: 323 Kentish Town Road, NW5 2AA
Station: Kentish Town
Also in: Multiple locations
Web: tonkotsu.co.uk

Toconoco

Casual Japanese cafe with play area

That its name is a made-up word meaning 'kids on the floor' tells you everything you need to know about this quirky cafe, which – true to its word – is often ankle-deep with infants. This, along with a lovingly hand-built play area, is testament to its relaxed vibe and child-friendliness, though the owner isn't keen on the term 'play cafe' (that, after all, might deter the cult following of laptop-tapping, dog-toting adults that flock here in pursuit of authentic, home-cooked Japanese fare). Such universal appeal speaks volumes though. The specials can sell out with lightning speed – though even if they have there'll still be plenty to tempt you. Fail-safe kid-pleasers include seaweed-wrapped rice balls and a matcha blondie whose deliciousness belies its rather unappetising shade of green, while grown-ups will go wild for the wasabi-avocado toast – a mouth-watering Japanese spin on a brunch classic.

NEARBY

Neighbouring Stonebridge Park is home to a locally famous mosaic snake climbing structure, while Dalston Eastern Curve Garden's colourful stage and assortment of love-worn ride-ons make it the perfect sunny-day hangout.

DETAILS

Facilities: Highchairs, baby change
Address: Unit A, 28 Hertford Road, N1 5QT
Station: Haggerston
Web: toconoco.com

Granary Square Brasserie

Modern British food in plush surrounds

With its giant crystal chandeliers, lush leather upholstery and near-excessive amounts of glass, this elegant King's Cross eatery may not feel like the most natural environment for young children, but give it a chance and it might surprise you. This former grain store feels anything but impersonal with its unflappable wait staff who always offer a smile and a colouring sheet for the kids. The eight-dish Little Dreamers menu borrows from the grown-ups but never once feels like an afterthought, with diminutive classics including chicken escalope and bangers and mash cooked to the same exacting standards as their adult equivalents. The real star, however, is the Dream Sundae, a ginormous platter of ice cream and DIY garnishes that's aptly named and well worth the sugar high.

NEARBY

Wellcome Collection, Francis Crick Institute and Queer Britain are all great spots to catch free exhibitions, while the Granary Square fountains are perfect for a quick splash on a hot day.

DETAILS

Facilities: Highchairs, baby change, kids' menu
Address: 1 Granary Square, NIC 4AB
Station: King's Cross
Web: granarysquarebrasserie.com

Caravan

All-day antipodean comfort eating

If Caravan were actually the size of a caravan, it would be a terrible place to take children. Thankfully it's absolutely massive, taking up a sizeable chunk of a former grain warehouse and having, if anything, more of an aircraft-hangar feel, with high ceilings that swallow shrieks and make you feel inconspicuous, even with the noisiest mob in tow. The menu, too, is ambitiously large (though, apparently, not enough to include a kids' section) and packed with all manner of delights that should suit the whole family, whatever the time of day. Feasting menus keep ordering simple, offering plenty for young ones and designed to be shared, while chewy sourdough pizzas are a similarly trustworthy shout. Feeling adventurous? The caramelised brioche with miso caramel offers just the right mix of sophistication and sweetness.

NEARBY

Caravan's outdoor seating is practically within toe-dipping distance of the Granary Square fountains, making them great for a post-lunch gambol while the adults finish their drinks. Or try the Lightroom for artist-led immersive cinema.

DETAILS

Facilities: Highchairs, baby change
Address: 1 Granary Square, NIC 4AA
Station: King's Cross
Also in: Multiple locations
Web: caravanandco.com

Franco Manca

Cheerful sourdough pizza chain

If we could only eat at a single restaurant for the remainder of our parenting journey, Franco Manca would be it. The fuss-free pizza chain began life in 1986 as the independent Franco's Pizzeria in what was then known as Brixton Market. Things have changed a bit since then, including a slight name alteration, a buyout, and the small matter of its massive expansion (there are now more than 70 Franco Mancas globally – half of them in London), but its commitment to exceptional sourdough pizza remains the same. And as for the ice cream machine, salad bar and dozens of other gimmicks popularised by similar big-name pizza chains? Well, you'll find none of that here – just friendly service, reasonable prices, a well-designed colouring sheet and pizza so good there's no (ahem) *topping* it. Keep an eye out during school holidays for offers that mean kids can eat for free.

NEARBY

The wild, open spaces of Hampstead Heath are just a short walk away, offering breathtaking views across London and a chance to view one of the world's most impressive collections of art at English Heritage-owned Kenwood House.

DETAILS

Facilities: Highchairs, baby change, kids' menu
Address: 216 Haverstock Hill, NW3 2AE
Station: Belsize Park
Also in: Multiple locations
Web: francomanca.co.uk

Megan's

Mezzes with holiday vibes

Even without the well-stocked toy box in the corner, this bright and breezy chain is a no-brainer for harassed parents of hangry tots thanks to its relaxed vibe, top-notch facilities and abundance of hummus. The loose Mediterranean theme extends beyond the menu, with lobster-pot lampshades and Moroccan tiles almost fooling you into believing you're on a break in Tangier, and not in a former Royal Mail sorting office in Islington. For little ones, there are pizzas, picking plates and pancake stacks, as well as the opportunity to bypass the kids' menu entirely in favour of an immensely shareable mezze platter, loaded with crunchy crudités, pitta strips and piles of fries. To finish, ask for the half-baked cookie-dough dessert and as many spoons as you deem necessary. Or linger over salted caramel martinis while the kids dig in to that toy box.

NEARBY

Poppets Stores play cafe serves good coffee, snacks and sandwiches in a friendly space with a playroom, garden and small shop. Molly Meg is Islington's go-to for stylish children's gifts, nursery furnishings and party provisions.

DETAILS

Facilities: Highchairs, baby change, kids' menu
Address: 6 Esther Anne Place, N1 1WF
Station: Essex Road
Also in: Multiple locations
Web: megans.co.uk

...aster egg coloured in, we...
...ool. Just give your egg to a...
...can get a real chocolate egg...

D...

...by ....

Beam

Middle Eastern brunch spot

True to its name, this dreamy cafe is a ray of light in an otherwise fairly cafe-sparse landscape – at least where very young ones are concerned. Middle Eastern in flavour, the much-loved hangout might do a roaring trade in tangy shakshuka and shawarma eggs Benedict (and with good reason), but there's still plenty here to tempt less sophisticated diners, from tiny portions of chicken nuggets and fish fingers to an extremely decadent Nutella French toast, perfect milk-shakes and an ever-changing line-up of freshly baked cakes. Add in ample highchairs and attentive service, and it's no wonder that this place is invariably groaning with families. Don't worry though – its stylish modern interiors, good strong coffee and small but decent drinks menu should keep the grown-ups positively *beaming*.

NEARBY

Clissold Park is a year-round treat, boasting 56 acres of green space; birds, goats and fallow deer; and a splash pad in the summer months. In the other direction, Islington's largest nature reserve, Gillespie Park, runs pond-dipping sessions for kids of all ages.

DETAILS

Facilities: Highchairs, baby change
Address: 184 Blackstock Road, N5 1EG
Station: Arsenal
Also in: Multiple locations
Web: cafebeam.co.uk

BAO

Idiosyncratic Taiwanese cafe

Wes Anderson vibes abound at this stylish steamed bun spot, whose delightful mid-century interiors may at first glance appear far too nice for your horrible children. But while aesthetics are important here, good service is more so – and that extends to said horrible children, who will be warmly welcomed by wait staff then guided through the most kid-friendly dishes on the menu. These include dangerously addictive dry-noodle snacks, a perfectly petite bowl of guinea fowl chi shiang rice, maple-smeared fries (enough said) and Bao's signature sad-face custard bun – star of many an Instagram feed. And let's not forget the main event: delicious mounds of perfectly seasoned pork, fish, beef, prawn or daikon, bookended by warm, fluffy bao (much like a burger, but better). Grab the tote while you're there – and look out for the impossibly cute limited edition buns.

NEARBY

Camley Street Natural Park offers two acres of wild green space next to St Pancras Lock, while the Grant Museum of Zoology is home to some of the world's rarest animal specimens.

DETAILS

Facilities: Highchairs, baby change

Address: Unit 2, 4 Pancras Square, N1C 4DP

Station: King's Cross

Also in: Borough, Soho

Web: baolondon.com

Mildreds

Plant-based plates

With its vibrant, nourishing food spanning tot-pleasing sides and extremely shareable desserts, the OG of vegan dining would be an excellent spot to eat out with little ones whether they had a children's menu or not. That they do, and it's brilliant, is a happy bonus that regularly sees the place packed with tiny vegans (or, at least, the off-spring of big ones) munching on miniature bowls of creamy coconut curry, colourful rainbow rice and chick'n nuggets and fries – all un-failingly scrumptious. Likewise, there's very little on the adult menu that's not worth ordering, but the banana Biscoff pancakes, tangy bokkeumbap and naughty BBQ pok bun are all delicious places to start and should keep you satisfied whether you're 100 per cent plant-based or significantly less.

NEARBY

Corams Fields is a year-round joy, offering seven acres of family-only parkland with several playgrounds and a paddling pool in the summer months. Or try the Postal Museum for endless interactives, Royal Mail-themed play and an underground train ride.

DETAILS

Facilities: Highchairs, baby change, kids' menu
Address: 200 Pentonville Road, N1 9JP
Station: King's Cross
Also in: Multiple locations
Web: mildreds.co.uk

German Gymnasium

Schnitzels and sausages

London's first purpose-built gymnasium is no longer a gymnasium, but rather its polar opposite: a place where you can stuff your face with all manner of potato-topped, meat-rich, gravy-laden mains and still be required to make space for a Black Forest gateau. This is all great news for beige-food-loving kids, who'll be in complex-carb heaven with their own dedicated menu filled with fat potato knödel (dumplings), crunchy schupfnudel (potato noodles) and crispy schnitzel with a side of uh… potatoes. Grown-up offerings err on the more adventurous side, but if you want authenticity, do as the Deutsch do and order a pickled herring, smoked sausage, or butcher's sharing plate stacked with all the sauerkraut, weisswurst and schnitzel you can fit in your kuchen-hole. Wunderbar!

NEARBY

Work off all those carbs with a frolic through the ever-popular Granary Square fountains or a wander around the Story Garden, a community-focused urban oasis. Or check out an often-interactive, always-informative free exhibition at the Francis Crick Institute.

DETAILS

Facilities: Highchairs, baby change, kids' menu
Address: 1 King's Boulevard, NIC 4BU
Station: King's Cross
Web: germangymnasium.com

Pizza Pilgrims

Crowd-pleasing pizzs with a basement gaming den

This cheery chain might have 17 branches across London, but this outpost is the only one with a gaming den in the basement. The fact that it's the capital's biggest, with plenty of space for highchairs and buggies, *and* right next door to family favourite Museum of London Docklands, makes it the obvious choice for (relatively) peaceful feasts with young ones. Kids can get in on the same adventurous pizza action as the grown-ups (yep, even the pepperoni and spicy honey and salsiccia e friarielli), only on a smaller scale, with mini ice cream sandwiches and their signature Nutella pizza rings for dessert. Give yourself extra time to enjoy the full array of retro games, which includes Donkey Kong, Pac-Man and foosball, for starters. Speaking of which, do yourself a favour and begin with the deep-fried artichokes fritti – you won't regret it.

NEARBY

There's always something to see in Canary Wharf, be it an interactive sculpture trail or artist-designed mini golf, while the aforementioned Museum of London Docklands offers free play sessions in its interactive gallery for 0-8s.

DETAILS

Facilities: Highchairs, baby change
Address: 12 Hertsmere Road, E14 4AE
Station: West India Quay
Also in: Multiple locations
Web: pizzapilgrims.co.uk

Koya Ko

Relaxed noodle bar with kids' trays

The family-friendly version of the famed Koya noodle bar ('ko' roughly translates as 'child') is, as you'd expect, a little more playful than its big sister. Gone is the slightly intense communal counter seating, the complete lack of buggy space and the feeling that a toddler tantrum probably wouldn't go down that well, and in its place is a dedicated kids' menu, adorable training chopsticks and a laid-back vibe to match its Broadway Market setting. You won't find much besides noodles here, but they're so satisfyingly slurpable you wouldn't want to – plus kids get a colouring sheet, veggie pot, drink of choice *and* a cup of (no bits) miso to accompany their steaming bowls of udon broth. Grown-ups, meanwhile, get to supplement their mains with piles of crispy tempura and tangy pickles, followed by a malty ice cream sandwich to seriously sweeten the deal.

NEARBY

The infinitely browsable Artwords will be a hit with bookworms young and old – though its children's selection is particularly well curated. Young V&A reopens in summer 2023, promising sensory playscapes, an Imagination Playground and a storytelling stage.

DETAILS

Facilities: Highchairs, kids' menu
Address: 10 Broadway Market Mews, E8 4TS
Station: London Fields
Also in: The City, Soho
Web: koya.co.uk

Sticks'n'Sushi

Cool Japanese with a warm welcome

Few cuisines are such unlikely child-pleasers as sushi, and yet we've never met a tot who wouldn't devour a dragon roll in 10 seconds flat. This upmarket Japanese is capitalising on kids' fondness for hand rolls with a family-friendly menu that belies its industrial-chic interior – though admittedly with a Studio Ghibli mural that somewhat gives it away. Kids' bento boxes bursting with veggie maki, chicken teriyaki and other inoffensive favourites offer a safe option for fussier eaters, though there's plenty on the main menu to satisfy tiny taste buds, from crisp tempura shrimp to comforting miso and various juicy morsels on sticks, all washed down with a shoal of chocolate fish and a sweet bottle of fizzy, lemonade-y ramune. Aspiring itamae in the family? Ask about Kids'n'Sushi rolling sessions for ages 8-12.

NEARBY

Stroll through the exotic plants of Crossrail Place Roof Garden, or head to the Museum of London Docklands for an interactive kids' gallery and regular family events. Meanwhile, Mudchute Park and Farm offers animal encounters and weekend loose-parts play.

DETAILS

Facilities: Highchairs, baby change, kids' menu
Address: 1 Crossrail Place, E14 5AR
Station: Canary Wharf
Also in: Multiple locations
Web: sticksnsushi.com

Poppies

Top-notch chip shop with wartime memorabilia

Think London fish and chips, think Poppies. The iconic chippy has been serving its premium take on the British classic for over a decade, while its founder, the eponymous Pat 'Pop' Newland, handed Londoners their newspaper-wrapped suppers for over seven decades. Everything about Poppies feels comfortingly old-school, from the kitsch collectables that adorn the walls to the bespoke packaging that comes plastered with historic headlines, and yet the fish is the freshest you'll find, arriving direct from Billingsgate Market every morning, ready to be slathered in Poppies' legendarily crispy batter. As for family-friendliness, pint-sized diners get their own dedicated menu featuring mini versions of Poppies' bestsellers, plus special treatment from the already super-attentive staff. Head down on the first Friday of the month and treat the whole family to a live gig while you gobble.

NEARBY

Hours of fun await at Camden's subterranean Babylon Park, which packs in an indoor rollercoaster, claw machines and colourful soft play. Or head to Social Pottery for a spot of paint therapy in a friendly studio with a huge choice of ceramics to decorate.

DETAILS

Facilities: Highchairs, baby change, kids' menu
Address: 6–8 Hanbury Street, E1 6QR
Station: Shoreditch High Street
Also in: Soho, Camden
Web: poppiesfishandchips.co.uk

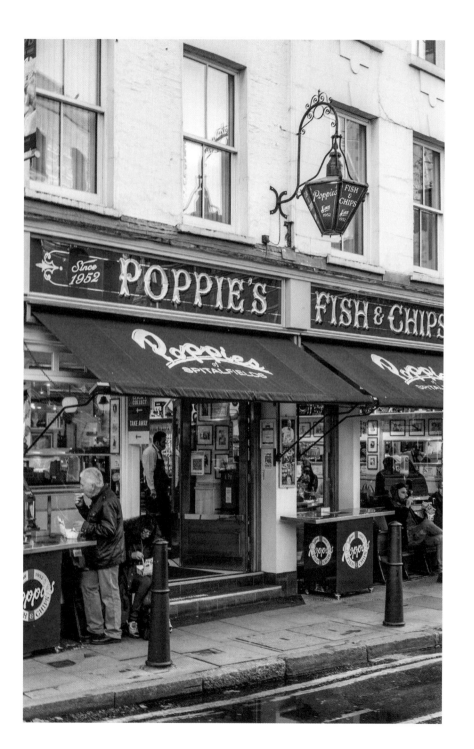

The Hub Cafe

Family favourites in an easy-going space

Eating out with young kids doesn't always feel easy, but at this mum-run park cafe it's a joy thanks to a well-conceived children's menu, kind staff and family facilities – which should be the bare minimum but in reality are so rare you're disproportionately (often embarrassingly) grateful when you find them. Meals are simple but well done, with topped sourdough toast, mini mezzes and pancake stacks for the kids, and cut-above continental breakfasts and brunches for the grown-ups (the crisp feta rostis and tasty huevos rancheros being particular favourites). The light bites are tempting too, comprising generous wedges of moist homemade cake, fat chocolate cookies and puffy pastries, alongside the usual pre-packaged pre-schooler favourites. The play area would benefit from a few flourishes, but the fact that there's one at all is a huge bonus – plus there's a huge playground outside for when they inevitably tire of it.

NEARBY

Victoria Park playground hosts a trio of giant hillside slides, a big wobbly bridge and an adjoining summertime splash pool. Up the road on Well Street, What Mother Made offers sustainable women's and kids' clothing with a vintage edge.

DETAILS

Facilities: Highchairs, baby change, kids' menu
Address: Victoria Park, Old Ford Road, E3 5PE
Station: Hackney Wick
Web: thehubvictoriapark.net

Mama Shelter

Refuel and recharge in a dreamy creative lounge

It might not be the meaning Serge Trigano had in mind when he dreamt up his Mama Shelter concept, but this welcoming hub certainly feels like a refuge for mothers (and fathers, and anyone else tasked with getting through a meal in the company of youngsters). Comfortable, relaxed and gorgeously eccentric, the space functions particularly well for those attempting to dine with young children, with sofas to laze (and, yes, eat) on, endless comics to peruse, arcade games to explore, a foosball table to tinker with and plenty to stare at while they eat, from vintage cartoons on loop to a galaxy of lamps. The main menu varies depending on when you visit, with recuperative brunches on weekends and indulgent roasts on Sundays, but the kids' offer is a reliable constant, packed with guaranteed crowd pleasers and reassuring home cooking – just like their mama makes.

NEARBY

Museum of the Home presents stories of homes through time in a thoughtful and engaging way, with plenty of interactives. Little ones will love Hackney City Farm with its menagerie of ponies, pigs, donkeys, goats, sheep and birds.

DETAILS

Facilities: Highchairs, baby change, kids' menu
Address: 437 Hackney Road, E2 8PP
Station: Cambridge Heath
Web: mamashelter.com

The Duke of Richmond

Hip neighbourhood gastropub

Celebrated chef Tom Oldroyd and his partner Meryl Fernandes know a thing or two about eating out with kids, having been custodians of this pub since 2018 and a small child for even longer. While not a 'family pub' in the usual, often quite awful sense, this stylish spot is still an excellent place to eat with children thanks to its obliging staff, reasonably priced kids' menu and general lack of hostility towards young ones (the pub has previously hosted a Mum and Dad Lunch Club and Drag Queen Storytime). For this venture, Oldroyd has created a meaty menu of groaning burgers, massive roasts and similarly substantial delights, including an Insta-famous crab and chip butty, while kids can choose from spaghetti or mini-burgers, and shrunken roasts on a Sunday. Or swing by on a Friday when they eat free of charge.

NEARBY

Release restless little ones into Dalston Curve Garden, where they can wrestle with all manner of ride-on toys or act out their own performances on the colourful stage.

DETAILS

Facilities: Highchairs, baby change, kids' menu
Address: 316 Queensbridge Road, E8 3NH
Station: Dalston Junction
Web: thedukeofrichmond.com

Flat Iron

Let them eat steak

It's never too early to encourage a love of steak. Or at least that's the philosophy at this popular chain, whose aim is to make tender, juicy cuts of beef accessible to everyone – including kids. There's no children's menu per se, but to be fair there's not much of an adult one either. Aside from the specials, which span burgers, sirloin and bavette, the mains menu comprises a single dish: an eponymous slab of steak served with your choice of sides and sauces. Still, there's plenty to appease kids who lack an appetite for the really meaty stuff, from beef-dripping chips to truffled mac and cheese. What might clinch it, however, are the popcorn and ice cream that bookend the meal (and what might sell it to *you* is that both come on the house). Just keep those meat cleavers out of reach.

NEARBY

The beautiful Boundary Estate has a fascinating history as one of the world's oldest social housing projects, and is home to Luna & Curious, a self-styled 'miniature department store' stocking stylish womenswear, kidswear and accessories from independent brands.

DETAILS

Address: 88–90 Commercial Street, E1 6LY
Station: Shoreditch High Street
Also in: Multiple locations
Web: flatironsteak.co.uk

Frizzante

Italian farm-to-fork fare

Hackney City Farm's rustic cafe attracts families almost – but not quite – to the exclusion of everyone else, thanks to its toddler-hotspot location and crowd-pleasing home cooking. While it often errs on the chaotic, particularly on weekday lunchtimes when little ones rule the roost, the upshot is an absence of parental judgement, since pretty much everyone else is in possession of their own little farmyard animal. Authentic Italian dishes showcasing locally sourced and homegrown produce dominate the menu, with hearty brunches, Mediterranean classics and perfect cannoli for the adults, and small portions of simple pasta, things on toast and homemade gelato for the wee ones. Add to that a changing daily selection of irresistible home bakes, copious snacks and ample outdoor frolicking space, and they should be as happy as pigs in the proverbial.

NEARBY

You categorically can't eat here without calling in to say hello to the menagerie next door. Once you're acquainted, let your brood run around like headless chickens in the playground on the far side of Haggerston Park.

DETAILS

Facilities: Highchairs, baby change, kids' menu
Address: 1a Goldsmiths Row, E2 8QA
Station: Cambridge Heath
Web: frizzantecafe.com

Wahaca

Food for thought

Producing Mexican-inspired food that's authentic *and* family-friendly is no mean feat, but Thomasina Miers and Mark Selby have done a fine job with their popular brand of Central American-style street eats, whose flavours elegantly straddle the line between adventurous and accessible. While the whole family will be keen to get their chops around Wahaca's deliciously crisp tacos, melty quesadillas, and jam-packed burritos, 0-8s can also order from their own mini menu, featuring deconstructed dishes that help them avoid the horror of unwanted ingredients on their plate or – that even greater toddler food faux pas – *things touching*. The restaurant's eco credentials up its family appeal even further, its ultra-transparent menu offering ample opportunity for discussions around sustainability, as well as more planet-friendly alternatives to carbon-heavy favourites – speaking of which, kids will go positively loco for the impossibly creamy Wahacamole dip and bottomless tortilla chips.

NEARBY

The Southbank Centre is famously great for kids, with a packed year-round programme of family events, stylish gift shop with a large children's selection, Little Library reading room and artist Jeppe Hein's summertime play fountain, Appearing Rooms.

DETAILS

Facilities: Highchairs, baby change, kids' menu
Address: Queen Elizabeth Hall, Southbank Centre, Belvedere Road, SE1 8XX
Station: Waterloo
Also in: Multiple locations
Web: wahaca.co.uk

Jefferson's

Contemporary ice cream parlour

'Gloriously Good' beams this adorable ice cream spot's logo, which takes the form of a smiley-faced bowl of the sweet stuff complete with scoops for hair. And we have to say, we're inclined to agree. Jefferson's has been sweetening the lives of south Londoners since 2019 with its intensely tasty, densely creamy brand of ice cream. Handmade in-house using natural ingredients, this flavour-packed, additive-free ambrosia is every kid's (and big kid's) fantasy, whether served straight up in a cone or cup, laden with all the sauces, sprinkles and sweets they can stomach, wedged between a pair of delightfully chewy cookies, or dolloped on steaming iron-fresh waffles – another of Jefferson's specialities. Keep an eye on their social media for news on madcap monthly specials – the perfect excuse for regular return visits.

NEARBY

With its entertaining slime show and collaborative 'giant' slime-making – plus loads of colourful slime to take home – there's a lot to love about Slime Planet. Or try Ritzy's Kids' Club cinema screenings featuring pre-film LEGO City workshops.

DETAILS

Facilities: Highchairs, baby change
Address: Arch 545 Brixton Station Road, SW9 8PF
Station: Brixton
Also in: Balham
Web: jeffersonsicecream.com

Where The Pancakes Are

Pancakes for every mood (even your three-year-old's)

Who said pancakes are just for Shrove Tuesday? Not this laid-back all-day breakfast, brunch, dessert and whatever-else-you're-calling-it spot, whose fluffy creations are so wildly inventive they're on a whole different planet to your traditional sugar- and lemon-topped treats – and so mind-blowingly delicious, Pancake Day will likely become a much more frequent celebration. While several of WTPA's offerings are on the more sophisticated side – think pastrami-topped pancakes with tangy slaw, or corn fritters piled with rocket and pickled lemons – most will appeal to younger palates. Portions are generous and ideal for sharing with tiny ones, while the build-your-own menu gives older kids free rein to experiment with whatever revolting combinations they wish (baked beans, sausage and maple syrup, anyone?). And should you desire more toppings, you're in luck: there's even a separate extras menu for when you're feeling particularly... well, extra.

NEARBY

Unicorn children's theatre stages trailblazing shows for ages 6 months to 12 years. The play fountains at More London are everything on blazing hot days, and offer unbeatable views of Tower Bridge and the Thames.

DETAILS

Facilities: Highchairs, baby change, kids' menu
Address: Arch 35a, 85a Southwark Bridge Road, SE1 0NQ
Station: Borough
Also in: Battersea, Fitzrovia
Web: wherethepancakesare.com

Mercato Metropolitano

Eclectic food market in former paper factory

The laid-back nature of multi-vendor food halls makes them perfect for beleaguered parents who don't fancy enduring the waiter's side-eye, or trying to persuade their kids to remain seated for the duration of a meal. This popular south London spot is particularly well suited to families, offering affordable eats from more than 40 kitchens spanning diverse cuisines, ample roaming space with pianos to poke while they await the trill of the buzzer, and probably more highchairs than we've ever clocked in a single space. There's no kids' menu as such, but most portions are small and shareable, with plenty to tempt even the fussiest little foodies. Why not sample Dez Amore's fresh pasta, Wrap Mi's fluffy bao buns or Fresco's perfectly chewy, gooey pizza – perhaps with a glass of hoppy happiness from on-site micro-brewery German Kraft Beer?

NEARBY

Elephant Park's cascading waterscape provides a spectacular setting for sunny-day play. In the cooler months, head to the Imperial War Museum and discover real stories of modern conflict via interactive exhibits.

DETAILS

Facilities: Highchairs, baby change
Address: 42 Newington Causeway, SE21 6DR
Station: Elephant and Castle
Also in: Multiple locations
Web: mercatometropolitano.com

BrewDog

Beer and buffalo wings beneath Waterloo station

That it has its own slide might be reason enough to take your children to London's biggest bar, but there's more to this Waterloo newcomer than slippery thrills. Take, for example, the mini bowling alley, stocked with lightweight balls that are perfect for tiny hands; or the on-site Hackney Gelato ice cream truck, which serves up doughnut sandwiches every hour of the day. The main menu is pretty good too, bursting with comfort food classics served in such generous portions you have to be careful when mixing them with beer for fear of inducing a carb coma (still, we heartily recommend the fiery Temple of Seitan wings and decadent loaded fries). You can even pick up ingeniously named kids' Hoppy Meal boxes complete with vegan burgers, crayons and a token for that ice cream truck. Far too tempting not to stay all day (and really, why wouldn't you?).

NEARBY

The delights of the Southbank know no bounds, spanning Tate Modern, the London Eye, BFI and Royal Festival Hall. Jubilee Gardens Playground is great for all ages, while older ones will enjoy interactive gaming at Immersive Gamebox and board games at Draughts.

DETAILS

Facilities: Highchairs, baby change, kids' menu
Address: Unit G, Waterloo Station, 01 The Sidings, SE1 7BH
Station: Waterloo
Web: brewdog.com

BOXPARK
Croydon

Street eats spanning global cuisines

While the developers of this buzzy food hall might have fallen somewhat short of creating the 'modern-day Covent Garden Piazza' they were aiming for, they certainly succeeded in producing a family-friendly space. The soft-play area may be gone, but the colossal variety of street eats (along with crafty Sunday fun courtesy of The Kids' Table) keeps families flocking back to this quirky arrangement of black shipping containers. It would be nigh on impossible to list all the kid-friendly fast food you'll find here, but gooey mac 'n' cheese croquettes from Nanny Bill's, crispy halloumi fries from Poptata and WOK's moreish pad Thai noodles are all good places to start – while naughty (but absurdly nice) vegan ice cream sandwiches from The After School Cookie Club and deep-fried mochi from Bao Bao are even better places to finish.

NEARBY

The recently renovated Queen's Gardens boasts two exciting play areas featuring a sunken trampoline and lofty play tower. Meanwhile, Kidspace's huge vertical labyrinth, interactive sandpit and terrifying slides are well worth the short bus ride.

DETAILS

Facilities: Baby change
Address: 99 George Street, CRO ILD
Station: East Croydon
Also in: Shoreditch, Wembley
Web: boxpark.co.uk

The Rosendale

Neighbourhood pub with playground

It's not every day you come across a London pub with its own play area, but the owners of this handsome former coaching inn have been kind enough to dedicate a sizeable chunk of their garden to its most impressionable customers. Here, pint-sized patrons can test drive colourful ride-ons or muck about on the wooden multi-play structure while they await their food – or even just while their grown-ups enjoy an al fresco drink in peace. The children's offer is essentially a condensed version of the main menu and features tiny editions of the least adventurously topped pizzas, mini portions of fish and chips, and small-plate versions of bestselling grown-up meals – including the epic Sunday roast. Make like a local and order a hoppy Gipsy Hill Hepcat IPA to start – but be sure to finish with the decidedly less regional espresso panna cotta.

NEARBY

Dulwich Picture Gallery's Mini Masterpieces sessions top the under-5s arty activity charts, and its family days are reliably good too. Paper Stories offers affordable collage packs that can be completed in-house over hot chocolate and cake.

DETAILS

Facilities: Highchairs, baby change, kids' menu
Address: 65 Rosendale Road, SE21 8EZ
Station: West Dulwich
Web: therosendale.co.uk

OXO Tower Restaurant, Bar & Brasserie

Elevated dining in an iconic building

It's hard to disassociate this elegant South Bank restaurant from the dried gravy brand, mainly on account of it being named after OXO... and having a huge tower with windows that quite literally spell it out for us. Those things aside, this eighth-floor favourite has very little to do with the brown stuff (perhaps, to your children's dismay), instead offering fun, fresh and highly inventive dishes, delivered by charming wait staff. Menus are seasonal, but vegetables are always the priority – even in the kids' menu, where they're cleverly concealed in sauces to relieve suspicion. Tiny hot dogs, popcorn-filled ramekins and wieldy plates of pasta make up the bulk of their fun but fail-safe menu, while grown-up highlights include beef cheeks and duck croquettes. The real star though has to be the view. The rest, as they say, is gravy.

NEARBY

Kids of all ages will love Jubilee Gardens playground, a substantial space in the shadow of the London Eye that offers ample opportunity for adventure. Or check out a contemporary art exhibition at the cavernous Tate Modern.

DETAILS

Facilities: Highchairs, baby change, kids' menu
Address: Barge House Street, SE1 9PH
Station: Blackfriars
Web: oxotowerrestaurant.com

OXO TOWER RESTAURANT
CHILDREN'S MENU

Choose a juice, starter, main and dessert 15

DRINKS
Choice of fresh juice: pineapple ₅₅kcal, apple ₉₀kcal, orange ₉₀kcal, tomato ₁₅kcal
cranberry ₈₅kcal

STARTERS
... am, salt and caramel ₂₆₀kcal
... ng sausages, sriracha mayo ₅₂₅kcal
... and mini pitta, harissa yoghurt (v) ₃₀₀kcal   ... ce, mozzarella, iceberg ₉₀kcal
                                                                  ... ʒm, basil, tomato sauce (ve) ₃₁₅kcal

112

Four Hundred Rabbits

Sourdough pizza to make you smile

Pizza joints might be two a penny in the capital, but this one is hard to forget, and not just because it has a silly name and decor that will remind you of school. Happily, the pizzas are memorable for all the right reasons, being simultaneously crisp and fluffy on the bottom and generously loaded up top, with inventive combinations spanning spicy vegan sausage and sriracha mayo, sweet and tangy pineapple and kimchi, and a chipotle-rolled goat's cheese and rhubarb that's particularly difficult to get out of your head. The kids' offer is a cautious mini-margherita-and-juice deal, though all pizzas come in half sizes for half the price, should they be feeling bold. Dessert is outrageously good gelato in a similarly creative array of flavours, with salted caramel and peanut a particular favourite. Regardless of what you order though, you can guarantee it won't be rabbit food.

NEARBY

Brockwell Park has it all, from a summer splash pad to a huge playground and even a miniature railway. Apple Tree Cafe offers soft play and themed activities for under-5s, while sustainable womenswear store Lowie is always worth a browse.

DETAILS

Facilities: Highchairs, baby change, kids' menu
Address: The Lido Cafe, Dulwich Road, SE24 0PA
Station: Herne Hill
Also in: Multiple locations
Web: 400rabbits.co.uk

Pear Tree Cafe

Trendy spot in popular park

Park cafes are the saviour of many a playground run. The purveyors of indispensable iced lattes and lollies on hot days and steaming hot chocolates on cold ones, not to mention the copious toddler snacks. And yet they're rarely the sort of places we'd think to bother with were we not already park bound. Battersea's chic lakeside cafe, however, is an exception to the rule. A spot we'd gladly grace for a lazy family brunch whether we were planning on visiting the playground or not (though you may have to at least agree to a pedalo ride if it's the latter). There's a (small) kids' menu but tots are generally happier nibbling on their adults' substantial portions of buttermilk pancakes or toast with spreads, or sharing a crusty sourdough pizza. Failing that, there's a better selection of cakes and snacks than most of the other park cafes we know put together.

NEARBY

There's loads to do in Battersea Park, from the sprawling playground with its collection of frankly terrifying slides to the children's zoo with its wildcats and tamarins, plus recumbent bikes, putt in the park, Go Ape, and boats for hire in the summer months.

DETAILS

Facilities: Highchairs, baby change, kids' menu
Address: Battersea Park, SW11 4NJ
Station: Battersea Park
Other location: Clapham Common
Web: peartreecafe.co.uk

Fiume

Thameside southern Italian delights

Fancy a slice of la dolce vita without straying beyond the M25? This ritzy Italian might be the closest you'll get to the real deal with its impressively authentic menu, waterfront views (fiume means 'river' in Italian) and generous concession for young diners – a hallmark of Mediterranean hospitality. Fluffy elliptical pizzas, substantial bowls of well-dressed pasta and an exhaustive selection of antipasti favourites make up the tempting main menu, while bambini are given a choice of trusty chicken meatballs, simple tagliatelle or a mini margherita, with a scoop of gelato as a sweetener (though don't be surprised if they'd rather share your decadently delicious Caprese chocolate cake). Head here in the warmer months, ask for a table on the spacious riverside terrace and prepare to be instantly transported to the shores of Lake Como (at least, if you squint).

NEARBY

The iconic Battersea Power Station is now a huge shopping and leisure destination offering lots for families, including mini golf at Birdies and a colourful playground at Prospect Place.

DETAILS

Facilities: Highchairs, baby change, kids' menu
Address: Circus West Village, SW8 5BN
Station: Battersea Power Station
Web: fiume-restaurant.co.uk

Pastaio

Pasta, but not as you know it

If you're questioning the merit of going out for pasta when you could just as easily make it at home, you probably haven't been to Pastaio. Located moments from Carnaby Street, this unfussy Italian works as well for impromptu post-shop carb stops as it does for special occasions thanks to its lack of a booking policy and simple but exceptional fare. Given the universal appeal of its main menu, Pastaio needn't have bothered with a kids' selection, but it's kind enough to offer one anyway – even if it is limited to half-size portions of its three simplest dishes, accompanied by crudités and washed down with a scoop of silky ice cream. Adults get more choice but should order the tempeh Bolognese or chilli and rocket spaghetti regardless – and must not under any circumstances miss out on the prosecco slushie.

NEARBY

Selfridges' toy department is the best in town, offering an inclusive selection of toys and games in a space so joyful you'll have to drag them away kicking and screaming. Or head to the Royal Academy of Art for world-class exhibitions and sell-out family workshops.

DETAILS

Facilities: Highchairs, baby change, kids' menu
Address: 19 Ganton Street, WIF 9BN
Station: Oxford Circus
Web: pastaio.co.uk

The Arber Garden

Upscale gastropub with a sustainable focus

Your search for a family-friendly central London pub ends at this Fitzrovia hotspot, which recently opened on the site of the former Middlesex Hospital. Named after and inspired by botanist and philosopher Agnes Arber, The Arber Garden offers modern British fare in a space befitting its name, with large picture windows and copious greenery giving the illusion of the outside creeping in. The food is comforting yet innovative, comprising revamped brunches, Sunday lunches and everyday classics, all made using sustainably sourced, seasonal produce, plus a reasonably priced kids' menu that's great provided your child isn't a vegetarian. On the whole it's hard to go wrong here, but whatever you decide on make sure it's accompanied by one of their fierce Bloody Marys and a fistful of crayons (find your colouring sheet on the back of the kids' menu).

NEARBY

The Cartoon Museum hosts insightful exhibitions in a playful space and runs brilliant holiday workshops for older children. Fitzrovia Children's Playground is open to the public on weekends and holidays, offering a tranquil but challenging haven for over–8s.

DETAILS

Facilities: Highchairs, baby change, kids' menu
Address: 1 Pearson Square, WIW 7EY
Station: Goodge Street
Web: thearbergarden.co.uk

Tapas Brindisa

Authentic tapas with Thames views

The riverside vistas glimpsed from Brindisa Richmond's elegant dining room are impressive, but probably not quite continental enough to convince your brain that you're feasting by the Med. The food, however, just might. Crisp Ibérico ham croquettes, juicy gambas and punchy patatas bravas are just a few of this authentic tapas joint's top picks, though with so many faithful favourites on the menu it's difficult to resist ordering it all. More adventurous young diners may prefer to share with the adults, while the niños menu offers milder takes on traditional Spanish dishes, from fluffy tortilla Española to creamy arroz meloso (and even chorizo and chips), along with a great selection of games and colouring activities to complete while they wait. And while *you* wait? Ask for a big, fizzy, fruity jug of Cava sangria. Salud!

NEARBY

Head to Richmond Park for breathtaking landscapes and more than 600 fallow deer. Or swing by kids' indie bookshop The Alligator's Mouth for regular author events, storytelling sessions and craft workshops.

DETAILS

Facilities: Highchairs, baby change, kids' menu
Address: 5 Whittaker Avenue, TW9 1EH
Station: Richmond
Also in: Multiple locations
Web: brindisakitchens.com

The Magazine

Seasonal food in deceptively friendly space

Turn up at The Magazine with a gaggle of hungry children and you'll immediately assume you've made some horrible mistake. Like a strange homage to *Logan's Run*, Zaha Hadid's Serpentine space is uncluttered, ultramodern and impossibly white – i.e., everything you've spent your entire parenting career avoiding. The service, thankfully, is so welcoming you'll soon stop caring and turn your attention instead to the intriguing Climavore menu, which takes its cues from the seasons and has been devised to minimise waste as much as possible (even if your toddler is dead set on doing the opposite). Perfectly blackened bonfire potatoes and satisfyingly savoury seaweed-dusted mussels are particular triumphs, while the children's menu should satisfy even the fussiest little feasters with top-notch fish fingers and creamy mac and cheese – which, by the way, they can splatter on those white surfaces as much as they like.

NEARBY

There's always something worth seeing at the Serpentine Galleries, be it cutting-edge VR exhibits or its annual pavilion. The Diana Memorial Playground's imposing pirate ship will thrill kids of all ages, while the fast-moving play fountain is extremely popular come summer.

DETAILS

Facilities: Highchairs, baby change, kids' menu
Address: Serpentine North Gallery, W2 2AR
Station: Lancaster Gate
Web: serpentinegalleries.org

Wands & Wizard Exploratorium

Spellbinding tea in a Soho townhouse

Like a touch of alchemy with your afternoon tea? This bewitching experience has it in buckets (or perhaps that should be cauldrons?), giving aspiring mages of all ages the chance to conjure their own tiny scones and rainbow macarons – though hopefully with no eye of newt or toe of frog poking out from their cucumber sandwiches. True to its name, Wands & Wizard offers magical beings young and old the opportunity to wield an enchanted (electronic) baton, harnessing its power to reveal secret ingredients, summon mystical assistants, and light up their table with colourful illuminations. Meanwhile, a dizzying variety of teas allow for some serious potion-making action – even if the flavours end up so muddled they're undrinkable. Craving more toil and trouble? Follow up with the Potions Experience and prepare to be spellbound.

NEARBY

The LEGO Store promises hours of fun with digital interactives, must-see installations, and brick-building tables galore. Or head to the Phoenix Garden, a gloriously green retreat that's handily located next to St Giles' Churchyard Playground.

DETAILS

Facilities: Highchairs
Address: 26 Greek Street, WID 5DE
Station: Tottenham Court Road
Web: wizardexploratorium.io

Apricity

Sustainable fine dining for foodies young and old

This reassuringly relaxed Mayfair spot is the only London restaurant to offer a children's tasting menu – and if that's not reason enough to drag the kids there, then perhaps its Michelin Green Star might sway you. Indeed, not only is chef and owner Chantelle Nicholson's food next-level delicious, gastronomically outstanding *and* surprisingly kid-friendly, it's eco-friendly too, with food waste kept to a minimum and produce sourced exclusively from sustainable suppliers. As you might imagine, the tasting menu is worlds away from your usual kids' offer, with flavourful kabocha squash and meaty oyster mushrooms providing an infinitely more sophisticated alternative to the ubiquitous fish fingers and chips, while a pink rhubarb granita and baked apple chouxnut might tempt them away from the all-you-can-eat ice cream machine for life (or, at least, one can hope). Keep an eye out for Chef Chantelle's popular cooking and learning sessions for eco-minded future foodies.

NEARBY

The Wallace Collection runs monthly hands-on Discovering Armour sessions, offering over-5s the chance to learn about and try on pieces from its arms collection. Or pop in to Selfridges' toy department for a play on the giant floor piano.

DETAILS

Facilities: Highchairs, baby change, kids' menu
Address: 68 Duke Street, W1K 6JU
Station: Bond Street
Web: apricityrestaurant.com

Marugame Udon

Relaxed ramen canteen

Eating out with young kids isn't always a picnic, but this playful Japanese chain is putting the fun back into family dining with its laid-back vibes and self-serve system that kids will lose their noodle over. Speaking of which, there are numerous udon bowls to choose from, while young ones can pick up a mini chibi bowl, carton of juice, colouring sheet and crayons all for under a fiver, making this one of the most affordable family spots in central London (that is, provided you don't overdo the extras, which is easier said than done once you've clocked the tempura selection). As for the kids, the creamy dorayaki pancakes, moreish mochi and absurdly good matcha soft serve are all at serious risk of inflating your bill – though since the latter is all you can eat, you'll probably let them off.

NEARBY

Hamleys runs regular in-store events, from meet and greets with favourite characters to puppet shows, seasonal fun and toy demonstrations. Fancy some grown-up window shopping? Head to Liberty for six floors of cutting-edge design.

DETAILS

Facilities: Highchairs, kids' menu
Address: 1–4 Argyll Street, WIF 7TA
Station: Oxford Circus
Also in: Multiple locations
Web: marugame.co.uk

Pho

Reliably restorative noodles

If you're looking for real-deal Vietnamese, head to Kingsland Road (AKA 'Pho Mile'), where a dozen authentic nhà hàng await your every bánh mì craving. Or, if you're after something a little more predictable, head to this cheery street-food chain, whose dishes are just as fresh and tasty as the genuine article but presented in a user- (and kid-) friendly way. For the grown-ups, there are crunchy vegetables snuggled in vermicelli nests, healthy rice bowls and the eponymous pho piled with herbs. Little ones are given a similar choice, albeit in smaller portions or in the form of a brilliantly conceived picking plate for under-2s. The best bit? It's all so healthy you can absolutely justify pudding. Choose from sweet and gooey banana fritters, perfect pandan waffles or Vietnamese affogato with condensed-milk ice cream.

NEARBY

W1 Curates offers an ever-changing roster of free immersive digital artworks in the basement of Flannels, while Monopoly Lifesized allows families with kids aged 5+ to complete escape room-style challenges themed around the board game.

DETAILS

Facilities: Highchairs, kids' menu
Address: 163–165 Wardour Street, W1F 8WN
Station: Tottenham Court Road
Also in: Multiple locations
Web: phocafe.co.uk

Darcie & May Green

Uplifting Aussie eats on a rainbow barge

Calling an antipodean restaurant 'laid back' may be a cliché, but nonchalance really is king at this Peter Blake-designed eatery, whose lazy all-day brunches, friendly servers, and the fact that it's literally floating down the canal (well, kind of) make it near-perfect for young families. Granted, you're still on a boat with small children, but provided they're not prone to legging it and you don't bring a buggy the size of a small yacht, it should all be plain sailing. There's no kids' menu per se, but the brunches are enormous enough to share with little ones – the fancy bacon roll and award-winning banana bread sandwich being particular winners. Still hungry? Daisy Green's luxury lamingtons are famous for a reason, while the epic Mars bar cheesecake is worth pushing the boat out for.

NEARBY

Puppet Theatre Barge productions blend traditional marionette puppets with progressive messages. Or check out GoBoat, whose self-drive boats allow groups of up to eight explore the canal with no previous boating experience.

DETAILS

Address: Grand Union Canal, Sheldon Square, W2 6DS
Station: Paddington
Web: daisygreenfood.com

Fallow

Sustainable fare in a buzzy Mayfair dining room

It would be easy to feel horribly guilty bringing small children, those habitual wasters of perfectly good food, to a place like Fallow, whose modus operandi is utilising the bits others waste. Then again, you could take your visit to this lively Mayfair spot, where ingredients are grown on the ceiling and chefs work in the open so they can't furtively bin things, as an opportunity for a (gentle) lesson on sustainability – which the knowledgeable wait staff will no doubt be happy to assist you with. As with the adult menu, whose biggest hits include a bowl of caramelised corn ribs (like spare ribs, but corn) and an entire cod's head, eye and all, the Mini Fallowers menu feels exciting but straightforward, comprising classics (bangers, burgers, fish fingers) done exceptionally well. So well, in fact, you can probably stop worrying about them wasting any of it.

NEARBY

Japan Centre stocks all the mochi, Pockys and Hello Kitty merch kids could dream of. The newly transformed National Portrait Gallery offers a variety of creative family events.

DETAILS

Facilities: Highchairs, baby change, kids' menu
Address: 52 Haymarket, SW1Y 4RP
Station: Piccadilly Circus
Web: fallowrestaurant.com

Lina Stores

Italian institution

Pasta fiend in the family? This stylish Italian knows a thing or two about the starchy stuff, having been in the business for nearly 80 years – first as a now-iconic deli peddling all manner of authentic produce, and latterly as a small chain of chic diner-style eateries, of which this is the most recent. Dishes are simple and satisfying – piles of spaghetti strewn with parmesan and neatly parcelled burrata ravioli. They're also surprisingly inexpensive given the elegant interior, which nods to Lina's heritage with mid-century furnishings and pistachio-green everything. Kids' meals are available off-menu so simply ask and you will receive a goofproof bowl of spaghetti or shapes, topped with a sauce of their choice. Then, supposing there's space, finish on a sweet note with a scoop of gelato and a bag (or three) of baiocchi from the counter.

NEARBY

In the warmer months, neighbouring Lewis Cubitt Park is scattered with loose parts that children can arrange into their own play landscapes, plus the adjacent play fountains are just as much fun and usually significantly less packed than Granary Square's.

DETAILS

Facilities: Highchairs, baby change, kids' menu
Address: 20 Stable Street, N1C 4DR
Station: King's Cross
Also in: Soho, The City, Marylebone
Web: linastores.co.uk

Petersham Nurseries

Afternoon tea in a magical setting

Tea at Petersham Nurseries' Teahouse is a pleasure wasted on the young, and yet they're unlikely to complain as they tuck into a mountain of heavenly honey-drizzled cocktail sausages and delectable buttercream-topped cupcakes, washed down with cloudy lemonade. The grown-up tea is, if possible, even more indulgent than the kids' version, with rustic goat's cheese and candied walnut tarts, sweet cassis and currant meringues, and Petersham's own (optional) rose-petal prosecco knocking some of London's better-known teas off their cake stands. Then there's the setting, whose bare earth floors, artfully distressed vintage tables and canopy of creepers is pure fairy-tale magic, with a hint of Miss Haversham via *The Secret Garden*. Speaking of which, the bewitching nursery grounds are a must for a post-tea family wander.

NEARBY

Richmond Park is home to more than 600 fallow deer, as well as a good playground that's close to Petersham. Or head back into Richmond along the Thames, swinging by The Alligator's Mouth for beautiful kids' books and author events.

DETAILS

Facilities: Highchairs, baby change, kids' menu
Address: Off Church Lane, Petersham Road, TW10 7AB
Station: Richmond
Also in: Covent Garden
Web: petershamnurseries.com

Image credits

Koya Ko (p.2) ©Martin Usborne; Granary Square Brasserie (pp. 4–5) ©Martin Usborne; Lina Stores (p. 6) ©Lina Stores; Megan's (p.7) ©Martin Usborne; Seven Dials Market (first image), by Matthew Ashmore / Alamy Stock Photo; (second image), photo courtesy of Seven Dials Market; (third image) ©Anton Rodriguez; Gloria, ©Joann Pai; RedFarm ©RedFarm; inamo ©Laurie Fletcher; Peppa Pig Afternoon Tea Bus ©Martin Usborne; Cafe Murano (all images) ©John Carey; Barbican Kitchen ©Elle Pickering; Bread Street Kitchen & Bar ©Martin Usborne; Dishoom ©Haarala Hamilton; Sweet Thursday (all images) ©Martin Usborne; Tonkotsu ©Tonkotsu; Toconoco (first image), by @_winnieq_; Toconoco (second and third images) ©Martin Usborne; Granary Square Brasserie ©Martin Usborne; Caravan (all images) ©Caravan Restaurants; Franco Manca ©Martin Usborne; Megan's ©Martin Usborne; Beam ©Beam; BAO ©Philipa Langley; Mildreds ©Mildreds Restaurants; German Gymnasium (all images) ©German Gymnasium, D&D London, 2023; Pizza Pilgrims ©Pizza Pilgrims / Xavier Buendia; Koya Ko ©Anton Rodriguez; Sticks'n'Sushi (first image), by Alexander Edwards for Sticks'n'Sushi; (second and third images), by Robin Skjoldborg for Sticks'n'Sushi; Poppies ©Robert Evans / Alamy Stock Photo; The Hub Cafe ©Martin Usborne; Mama Shelter ©Mama Shelter London; The Duke of Richmond ©Orlando Gili; Flat Iron ©Martin Usborne; Frizzante ©Martin Usborne; Wahaca ©Charlotte Nott-Macaire; Jefferson's ©Adam Luszniak Photography; Where The Pancakes Are ©Where The Pancakes Are; Mercato Metropolitano ©Mickey Lee / Alamy Stock Photo; BrewDog ©Martin Usborne; BOXPARK Croydon ©Xavier Buendia; The Rosendale (first, third and fourth images) ©David Griffen; (second image) ©Naomi Gabrielle Photography; OXO Tower Restaurant (first image) ©Hoberman Publishing / Alamy Stock Photo; (second image) ©OXO Tower Restaurant; Four Hundred Rabbits ©Nic Crilly Hargrave; Pear Tree Cafe, by @pear.tree.cafe and @g.visuaals; Fiume ©Fiume, D&D London 2023; Pastaio (first image) ©Charlie McKay; (second and third image) ©Joe Woodhouse; The Arber Garden ©The Arber Garden; Tapas Brindisa (first and third images) ©Giles Christopher; (second image) ©Steven Joyce; The Magazine ©Elle Pickering; Wands & Wizard Exploratorium ©Wizard Afternoon Tea at the Wands & Wizard Exploratorium. Soho, London. Apricity ©Emmy Watts; Marugame ©Jamie Orlando Smith; Pho ©Martin Usborne; Darcie & May Green (first and second image) ©Melisa Coppola; (third image) ©Daisy Green Collection; Fallow ©Fallow Restaurant; Lina Stores ©Rebecca Hope; Petersham Nurseries ©Andrew Montgomery.

Eat Out in London With Kids
First edition

Published in 2023 by Hoxton Mini Press, London
Copyright © Hoxton Mini Press 2023. All rights reserved.

Text by Emmy Watts
Copy-editing by Octavia Stocker
Additional design by Richard Mason
Production by Sarah-Louise Deazley
Production and editorial support by Georgia Williams

With thanks to Matthew Young for help developing the series design.

A CIP catalogue record for this book is available from the British Library.

ISBN: 978-1-914314-42-1

Printed and bound by Finidr, Czech Republic

Hoxton Mini Press is an environmentally conscious publisher, committed
to offsetting our carbon footprint. This book is 100 percent carbon compensated,
with offset purchased from Stand For Trees.

For every book you buy from our website, we plant a tree:
www.hoxtonminipress.com

FSC
www.fsc.org

MIX
Paper from
responsible sources
FSC® C014138